THE STAR WARS

QUESTION and ANSWER BOOK about SPACE

Random House New York

Illustrated by
DAVID KAWAMI

Written by
DINAH L. MOCHÉ, Ph.D.
Associate Professor of Physics
Queensborough Community College of the
City University of New York

Special thanks to:

Robert J. MacMillin
Senior Information Specialist
NASA/Jet Propulsion Laboratory
Pasadena, California

Milton E. Reim and Terry White
Public Information Specialists
NASA/Johnson Space Center
Houston, Texas

David W. Garrett
Public Affairs Officer
Nicholas Panagakos
Public Affairs Director
NASA Headquarters

Peter W. Waller
Public Information Office
NASA/Ames Research Center
Moffett Field, California

Photograph and Illustration Credits: American Museum of Natural History/Hayden Planetarium, 37; Stephen Benton, "Crystal Beginning," 1976. Photo by Stephen Benton. Courtesy, Museum of Holography, New York City, 53; Copyright by the California Institute of Technology and the Carnegie Institution of Washington. Reproduced by permission from the Hale Observatories, title page, 36, 40, 45, 46, 49, 50; Erich Hartmann/Magnum Photos, Inc., 53; Jet Propulsion Laboratory, 19; National Aeronautics and Space Administration, 13, 18, 20, 21, 22, 24, 25, 26, 27, 28, 30, 32, 34, 35, 36, 37, 39, 42, 43, 51, 54, 55, 56, 57, 58, 59, 60; Novosti from Sovfoto, 23; Tass from Sovfoto, 41, 54; Frank "Shorty" Wilcox/The Image Bank, 12.

Library of Congress Cataloging in Publication Data
Moché, Dinah. The Star Wars question and answer book about space. SUMMARY: Answers frequently asked questions about life on other planets, survival in outer space, astronomy, space, exploration, and astronautics. 1. Astronomy—Juvenile literature. 2. Life on other planets—Juvenile literature. 3. Astronautics—Juvenile literature. [1. Astronomy. 2. Life on other planets. 3. Astronautics. 4. Questions and answers] I. Title. QB46.M72 520 78–19684 ISBN 0–394–84053–4 ISBN 0–394–94053–9 lib. bdg.
Manufactured in the United States of America   1 2 3 4 5 6 7 8 9 0

Photograph on the title page: Great nebula in Orion.

Star Wars introduces you to the fascinating worlds beyond Earth, beyond the moon, beyond the stars...deep into space!

Is there life in outer space? What lies beyond our solar system? Are space creatures trying to contact us? Can humans look into a past time?

The answers to these and many more questions about space are in this book. There are full-color photographs of galaxies, planets, stars, and robots. There's even information on how you can become a space explorer.

Is there intelligent life in outer space?

Probably! Scientists don't know, but they have been searching for years for life in space. They haven't been successful yet, but people continue to imagine what space creatures might look like. Science-fiction writers have invented all kinds of space creatures—Martians, little green men (L.G.M.), space people, and many, many others.

KAWAMI

Where could life exist in space?

Our sun is a star. It is the center of our solar system. Nine planets move around it in oval paths—orbits. Earth is one of these planets. Some planets have moons circling them. One or more of these planets or moons may have some forms of life on them.

Many stars besides our sun may have planets, some with moons. Maybe these planets and moons could support intelligent life.

Life could not exist on the stars because they are huge, hot balls of gases. And no life could exist in the empty spaces between the stars.

Would space creatures look like humans?

Not necessarily. They might look very different from us. Thousands of non-human things live on Earth—plants, bees, bacteria, and more. Many, many other things might live on other planets or their moons.

There might be very tiny beings with intelligence. Or maybe there are supergiants. Space creatures might live in water or crawl around or even fly.

Could space creatures be as smart as we are?

They could be even smarter! Humans have been on Earth just a few million years. Parts of space are much older than Earth. Intelligent life might have existed there long before humans.

Today we know many scientific facts that our ancestors didn't know. People who live after us will know even more. Creatures elsewhere in space may have existed long enough to learn more than we have.

How would we talk to space creatures?

If space creatures do exist, they might have languages that are very different from ours. However, all intelligent creatures probably understand the same simple mathematical codes. These might be a universal language. Radio waves can carry coded messages to and from Earth through outer space.

How might we contact space creatures?

The best way would be by radio signals. Radio waves are pulses of electricity that zoom through space at the fastest possible speed—the speed of light. Light travels at 186,282 miles (299,800 kilometers) a second. Of course, the radio in your bedroom can't be used for this kind of communication.

Radio telescope in the VLA.

What is a radio telescope?

A radio telescope has a large, dish-shaped receiver that collects radio signals from outer space. Its antenna can pick up radio signals from some stars and planets. The radio telescope can determine the location of these stars and planets.

What is our most powerful receiver for space messages?

The Very Large Array (VLA) in New Mexico is our most powerful receiver for radio signals from space. It has a number of radio telescopes that work together as a supertelescope. By 1981, it will have 27 radio telescopes, all linked with computers.

Are space creatures trying to contact us?

We haven't picked up any signals from them yet. Radio telescopes are usually too busy doing other research to listen for a message from space. But American scientists now think it's worthwhile to conduct a program to search for space messages. It is called Search for Extraterrestrial (beyond Earth) Intelligence—SETI. It is one of many programs run by NASA (National Aeronautics and Space Administration), a U.S. government agency.

If radio telescopes were pointed in the right direction at the right time and were tuned to the right channel, they could pick up a radio message from space creatures.

Where is the largest radio telescope on Earth?

On the island of Puerto Rico. It is built into a natural bowl in the mountains near Arecibo (ahr-uh-SEE-boe). Its dish-shaped receiver is 1,000 feet (305 meters) across.

Equipment to receive and send radio signals weighs 600 tons and is built high in the air above the receiver. The equipment is steered by motors and pointed by remote control. One scientist can operate all the equipment!

Bird's-eye view of the radio telescope at Arecibo.

Have we sent any messages into space?

Yes, but just one. In 1974, when the giant Arecibo radio telescope was improved, a celebration was held. At that time a coded message was radioed from it toward a distant cluster of stars.

The message began with a lesson explaining the code. Then it told about humans, our home planet, our solar system, and the telescope itself that beamed the message.

The Arecibo message will reach its target in 24,000 years. If it is picked up and answered right away, we'll receive that star message in 48,000 years!

Why aren't we sending more messages into space?

Some people fear that if we send out too many messages, we could be invaded by space creatures. Real star wars are very unlikely. But it is not entirely impossible for unfriendly space creatures to invade Earth.

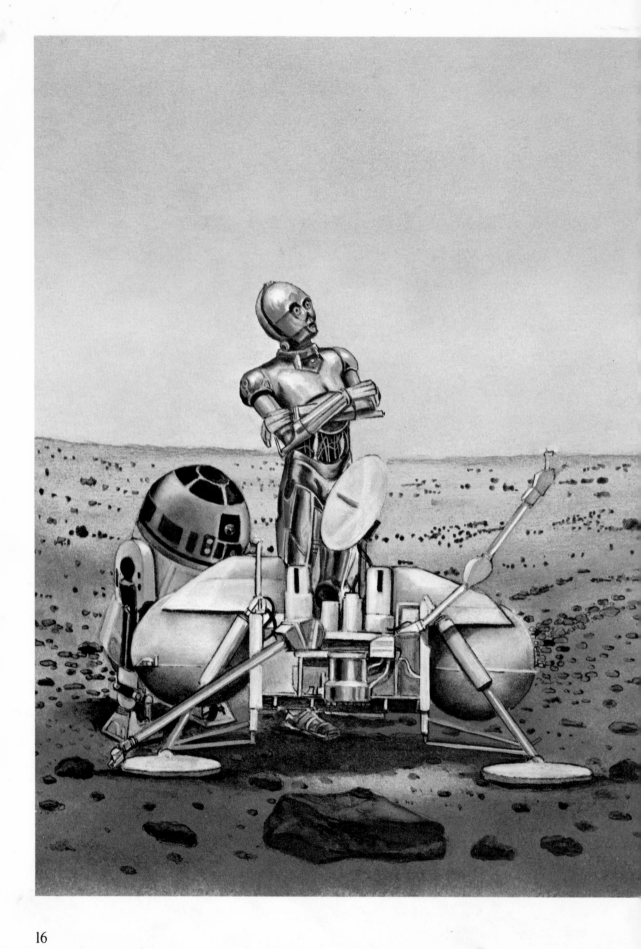

Are UFOs from outer space?

The people in charge of space exploration don't think so. They doubt that UFOs—Unidentified Flying Objects—are alien spaceships with live or robot space explorers inside. If they were, scientists would almost surely have discovered them by now.

In 1969 the U.S. Air Force ended its big, expensive 22-year-long investigation of UFOs, Project Blue Book. Even after following up more than 12,000 reports of UFOs, the air force had no positive scientific explanation for any of them. In 1977 President Carter's science adviser asked NASA to reopen a government investigation of UFOs. NASA said no—that it would probably be a waste of time and money.

What are UFOs?

No one knows for sure. But often UFO sightings are really the planet Venus shining brightly in the early evening. Sometimes a UFO is a bird flying at sunset or a U.S. Air Force craft or even a weather balloon. But not all UFO sightings have been explained.

Did space creatures visit Earth long ago?

There is no proof of it. Some ancient structures do look as if more knowledge was needed to build them than we think people had way back then. But each time scientists check on something we think may have been built by space creatures, they find that humans did have the knowledge and skill to do the work. Records show that people in ancient times knew many things about mining, transporting, and building.

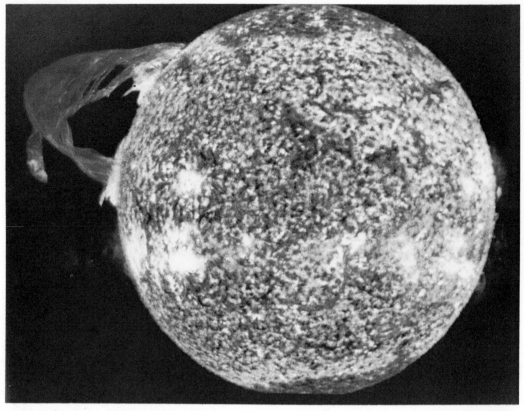

Solar flares.

Which star is closest to Earth?

Our sun! It is about 93 million miles (almost 150 million kilometers) away. Sunlight takes a little more than 8 minutes to travel to Earth. Many stars are probably like the sun. But our sun is the only star close enough to see well. If it were as far away as many other stars, you could not see it at all!

How does the sun affect Earth?

Our sun provides the heat and light that living things on Earth need. Tiny bits of gases on the sun move around very fast. They crash and stick together. Energy—heat and light—is freed.

Changes on the sun may affect Earth's climate and weather. Sudden flares send strong blasts of electric energy to Earth. They can disturb radios and compasses. They can cause the northern lights—the aurora borealis (aw-RAWR-uh bawr-ee-AL-iss)—to glow colorfully in the sky.

The sun's gravity pulls on Earth and the other planets. It keeps the planets in orbits around the sun.

Will the sun always shine?

No. But it will probably shine for another 5 billion years. Scientists think that at that time the center of the sun will shrink and become hotter. It will start using up the gases it needs for making energy. Then the sun will get bigger. Earth will get hotter and hotter, and all life on our planet will die. When the sun has used up its fuel, it will shrink. After billions of more years, it will stop shining.

Can people travel to the sun?

No. The sun is much too hot for people to go there. But we have sent spacecraft without people to explore the sun. NASA and the European Space Agency are planning a joint mission to send two spacecraft without people to the sun. They will explore the parts of the sun called the polar regions, and nearby space. The spacecraft will be named Solar Polar spacecraft.

Painting of spacecraft that will fly over solar poles.

How far have humans traveled into space?

The farthest humans have gone so far is to our moon, about 240,000 miles (384,000 kilometers) away. Neil Armstrong was the first person to set foot there, on July 20, 1969. Twelve astronauts landed on the moon in the Apollo moon missions between 1969 and 1972. They set up science experiments there, and they brought back 843 pounds (382 kilograms) of moon rocks for study on Earth.

Are there moon creatures?

The Apollo astronauts did not find any living creatures or plants on the moon. Scientists also did not find any fossils—traces of living things—in the moon rocks they brought back. The moon has no water or atmosphere (air), which plants and animals need to live. So future moon missions probably will not find life there either.

Why are moon rocks important in the search for life in space?

Moon rocks are made of the same chemical elements as Earth rocks, although the amounts of these elements are different. These elements are the same ingredients that living things are made of! Maybe these ingredients also exist on another moon or planet. If the conditions are right there, maybe they could develop into living creatures as they did on Earth.

Opposite: Photo of far side of moon taken from Apollo 8 spacecraft.
Inset: Astronaut Edwin Aldrin descending to the moon's surface.

Close-up photo of Apollo 15 lunar sample.

Photo of a thin section of Apollo 17 lunar sample taken through a microscope.

Painting of the surface of Venus.

Is there life on Venus?

We don't think so. The temperature there is 900° F (480° C). The atmosphere is mostly carbon dioxide. Our animals and plants couldn't live on Venus.

The Soviet spacecraft Venera 9 sent back the first picture of the surface of Venus in 1975. Eight robot spacecraft have tried to land there. But none of them has survived much more than an hour.

Two spacecraft named Pioneer Venus 1 and 2 are searching the clouds that surround Venus in 1979. They are not landing to look for living things because there probably aren't any.

Painting of Pioneer Venus 1 entering the atmosphere of Venus.

Have robot spacecraft landed anywhere in space?

Yes. Three Soviet robot spacecraft named Luna have visited our moon. They each brought back small samples of moon soil for scientists to study.

Two amazing American robots—Viking 1 and 2—landed on our neighbor planet Mars. Viking 1 and 2 carried out the first tests for living things ever done on another world.

Luna 16.

Photo of Martian landscape taken by the Viking 2 lander, with the lander in the foreground.

How did the Viking robots test for life on Mars?

Each robot had a long arm with a shovel at the end. It scooped up Martian soil and dumped it into a Biology Instrument it carried.

The Biology Instrument was really three complete biology labs. Though it was crammed into a package the size of a typewriter, it had 40,000 parts!

Plants and animals on Earth take in food and gases, use them to grow, and give off waste products. The Biology Instrument tested for those kinds of life signs in the Martian soil.

Did the Viking robots do anything else?

Yes. Photographs were taken of the Martian landscape and sent back to Earth. Equipment recorded the movements of the ground, and weather stations took air temperatures.

The robots' computers recorded the information on magnetic tape. News of their findings was sent back to Earth. The messages were picked up by radio telescope.

Opposite: Painting shows paths of commands that traveled to Mars from Earth (green), and information that was beamed back to Earth (purple).   *Inset:* Painting of arm that scooped up Martian soil for analysis.

How did the Viking robots get to Mars?

The robot lander was only one part of the Viking 1 and 2 space missions. The lander part of the Viking robots separated from the orbiter and touched down on the Martian surface. While it did tests on Mars, the orbiter part kept circling the planet. A camera in the orbiter took long-distance photographs of the surface of Mars.

Paintings of the landing sequence of the Viking 1 lander.

What did the Vikings see on Mars?

The orbiters photographed huge volcanoes, deep canyons, wild dust storms, and deep, winding channels that looked like dry riverbeds.

The Viking landers saw a bright-red desert scene. There were scattered rocks, sand dunes, and low hills in the distance. There was no flowing water. The daytime sky was pink. Sunsets were pale blue.

Why did the Vikings look for living things on Mars?

The dry, deep, branching channels on Mars look as if they were carved out by mighty rivers. Mars is very, very cold now. But perhaps it was once warm and had great rivers. If there was ever water on Mars, living things could have developed there. Maybe some have survived to this day.

Are there any Martians?

No one knows for sure. The Viking cameras did not photograph any creatures. The results of the soil tests for tiny living things are puzzling. Scientists are working on the puzzle in labs on Earth. Maybe new robots will go to Mars and gather more information.

Photo of Mars taken by Viking 1 orbiter.

Painting of the Viking orbiter as it passes over the robot lander.

Where are the Viking robots now?

The Vikings finished their search for living creatures on Mars in 1977. There are no plans to bring them home. The Viking landers will remain at their landing sites on Mars.

Can humans explore Mars?

Possibly. Mars is a rough, dry world. Its thin air is mostly carbon dioxide gas. Deadly radiation (rays) from the sun strikes the ground.

Mars is very cold. When Viking 1 landed there on July 20, 1976, the highest temperature it recorded was −22°F (−30°C). Winter temperatures went way below the lowest ever recorded on Earth. Humans could survive on Mars only if they had food, water, and a spacesuit.

The next astronauts on Mars will probably be robots. They are easier and cheaper to send than humans.

Painting of Viking lander taking soil samples.

Can robots think?

A robot's computer "brain" can be programmed (given coded instructions) to imitate thinking. The computer can take in information and decide how the robot will act. Computers can make robots do hard math problems quickly, write music and poems, and play chess—even learning to try harder to win! But humans still decide what goes into the computers and therefore what the robots do.

28

Can robots help each other?

Robots can be programmed to check on each other. Two robots might go together to explore Mars. If one has trouble, the other will signal Earth for help. Instructions can be sent from Earth to solve the problem.

How do robots get their energy?

Robots get their energy from electricity. On Earth, they can be plugged into electric outlets. Some robots that work far away from Earth have panels that catch sunlight and change it into electricity. Others use nuclear power to create electricity.

The Viking robots that landed on Mars were powered by nuclear energy. The orbiter that circled the planet had panels to trap sunlight for energy.

What do meteorites tell about life beyond Earth?

Meteorites are chunks of rock from outer space that land on Earth. Besides moon rocks, they are the only things from outer space that scientists have been able to examine. The Murchison meteorite that fell in Australia in 1969 contained amino acids. Amino acids are some of the basic materials that make up living things on Earth.

What is an asteroid?

An asteroid is a chunk of rock that circles our sun. Scientists have named and numbered more than 2,000 asteroids. The largest is named Ceres (SEER-eez). Ceres is as big across as Texas.

There are probably millions of small asteroids circling our sun. Most of them are found between the orbits of Mars and Jupiter.

Painting of spaceship journeying through the asteroid belt.

What would happen if an asteroid crashed into Earth?

Sometimes one of a small group of asteroids, called Apollos, crosses Earth's path in space. Most Apollos are less than a mile (about 1 kilometer) across. But if one crashed into Earth, it could scoop out a deep hole, big enough to hold New York City.

Fortunately such a crash is not likely to occur for millions of years.

Painting of Saturn as viewed from the moon Titan.
Inset: Photograph of the planet Saturn taken from Earth.

Which moons might have creatures living on them?

Titan, the giant moon circling Saturn, is the likeliest. Titan's clouds seem to be made of the same materials that blanketed Earth billions of years ago. These clouds may keep the surface of Titan warm and comfortable. It is possible that some tiny forms of life exist there.

Two robot spacecraft named Voyager 1 and 2 were launched in 1977. Their 12-year schedule includes taking a look at moons circling Jupiter (in 1979) and at Titan and other moons of Saturn (in 1980 and 1981).

Where does our solar system end?

Pluto, our sun's farthest planet, is 4 billion miles (6 billion kilometers) away from the sun. It is 40 times farther from the sun than Earth is. No spacecraft has gone there yet.

Pluto is so far away that it is just a dot in photographs taken through our largest telescopes. So it will be a long time until we have facts about this unknown little world at the edge of our solar system.

Which planets besides Earth have moons?

So far scientists have discovered that Mars has 2 moons, Jupiter appears to have 14, Saturn has 10, Uranus has 5, Neptune has 2, and Pluto appears to have 1.

The largest moon of all is Titan, which circles Saturn. It is wider than the United States. It is even bigger than the planet Mercury.

Can we explore outside our solar system?

Yes. We can send spacecraft without people beyond our solar system. Pioneer 10 took fantastic pictures of Jupiter in 1973. Pioneer 10 is still traveling and in 1987 it will become the first object made by humans ever to leave our solar system. It will not be able to send messages back. Pioneer 10 has a plaque with a picture message from us to any intelligent space creatures who see it.

In the 21st century we may send spacecraft to look for planets near the stars closest to our solar system.

Painting of Jupiter and four of its moons.

What do space missions tell space creatures about Earth?

Four space missions are carrying messages from humans to space creatures. If space creatures ever come across Pioneer 10 and 11 (Jupiter missions in 1973–74), they will find pictures of humans and planet Earth.

Voyager 1 and 2 were launched in 1977 to photograph Jupiter, Saturn, probably Uranus, and possibly Neptune. They carry more complicated information. Each one has a recording with two hours of coded Earth pictures and sounds, including animal noises and greetings from humans in 60 languages. Equipment for playing the record is included.

Model of the Voyager spacecraft.

Gold-plated "Sounds of Earth" record
that was placed aboard Voyager 2.

Will the Pioneers and Voyagers return to Earth?

Pioneer 10 and 11 and Voyager 1 and 2 will never return to Earth. They will coast through space forever. Perhaps they will, by chance, meet intelligent creatures who can understand their messages.

Spiral Galaxy.   Great Galaxy in Andromeda.

What lies beyond our solar system?

The stars! Long ago, people gave names to the brightest stars. Beginning in ancient times, people also named groups of stars—constellations—appearing close together in the night sky. The names came from shapes the stars seemed to make. Many of the names are people, animals, and things in ancient myths and legends. Astronomers (scientists who study the stars) now call each star by a letter of the Greek alphabet or a number, plus the constellation the star is in.

What is a galaxy?

A galaxy is a gigantic star system. The smaller galaxies have several hundred million stars. The largest have a thousand billion stars. All the stars in the galaxy, along with some gas and dust, move together through empty space.

How many galaxies are there?

Space seems to have more galaxies than we can count—maybe 100 billion of them! All other galaxies are very far away from the one in which we live. Photographs taken with powerful light telescopes show them as bright islands amid the vast darkness of space.

We can see only one big galaxy without a telescope. This galaxy—the Andromeda (an-DRAHM-uh-duh) Galaxy—really shines brighter than 100 billion suns. It looks like a tiny faint cloud because it is trillions of miles away from us.

In which galaxy is Earth?

The Milky Way Galaxy. Our sun and the whole solar system are, too. So are the stars and the milky band of starlight—called the Milky Way—you see in the night sky.

The Milky Way Galaxy is huge. We couldn't get beyond it even if we traveled a whole lifetime. A beam of starlight needs 100,000 years to travel from one side of our galaxy to the other!

Most of the stars in our galaxy are located in a flat spiral pattern with a bulge at the center. If we could see it from above, it would look like sparkles in the grooves of a phonograph record. The whole galaxy spins around slowly. It takes Earth along like a speck of dust. We can't notice this motion. It takes 250 million years for Earth to complete one circle.

How many stars are in our Milky Way Galaxy?

One hundred billion stars! If you gaze at the sky in a place where the sky is really dark and clear, you can see about 2,000 of these stars. Each one is an enormous ball of very hot gas. More than a million planets like Earth could fit inside an ordinary star. The stars you see look tiny only because they are very, very far away.

Painting of the Milky Way Galaxy.
Inset: Earth, a small speck in the Milky Way Galaxy, as photographed from Apollo 17.

How are space distances measured?

A unit called a light-year is used to measure distances to the stars. It is the distance that light, traveling 186,282 miles (299,800 kilometers) a second, can go in a year. That amounts to almost 6 trillion (6,000,000,000,000) miles, more than 9 trillion kilometers!

The distance to our neighbor galaxy, Andromeda, is 2 million light-years. That means a spaceship leaving Earth and zooming through space at light-speed would take 2 million years to get to the Andromeda Galaxy!

How far apart are the stars in our galaxy?

Stars are widely scattered about 5 light-years apart in our Milky Way Galaxy. Imagine that our sun (the closest star to Earth) is the size of a soccer ball. The closest star to the sun would then be the size of a soccer ball about 5,000 miles (8,000 kilometers) away.

What is between the stars?

Almost nothing is between the stars. Because there is no air, and thus no oxygen, you could not live there outside a spaceship without a spacesuit.

Material found between the stars is mostly hydrogen (HIE-druh-jin) gas. Some parts of our galaxy have huge gas and dust clouds, called nebulas (NEB-you-luhz). Some nebulas glow in brilliant colors as starlight passes through them. Others form weird dark shapes that block our view of distant stars.

Astronomers have found many different kinds of materials in these nebulas. They are important because new stars, planets, and perhaps living things are formed from nebulas.

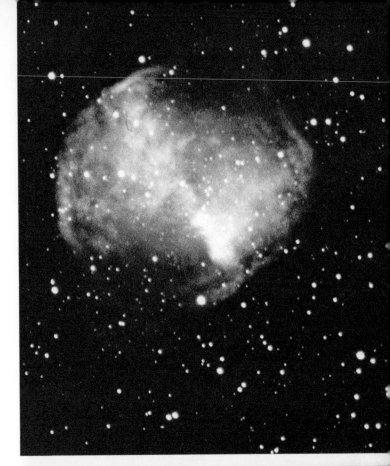

Nebulas.

Pleiades and nebulosity in Taurus.

How many other planetary systems might be in our galaxy?

There are probably billions! Astronomers think that our sun with its nine planets was formed out of a huge shrinking cloud about 5 billion years ago. Our sun is an ordinary star. Our galaxy has 100 billion stars. Many other suns with planets possibly were formed the same way.

How close could our nearest intelligent neighbors be?

The most hopeful scientists figure that a million planets in our galaxy have intelligent beings. If that's so, then our nearest intelligent neighbors could be just a few light-years away. It is much more likely that they are within 100 light-years of Earth than farther away. Still, that is an impossible distance for us to travel now.

Can humans see planets circling other stars?

No, not even with our largest telescopes. All stars are very far away. Planets are much smaller than stars and shine by reflecting starlight. A star greatly outshines its planets.

Since astronomers can't see another star's planets, they look for clues that planets exist. Like the sun's planets, those of another star would pull on the star as they circle it. So astronomers watch for wobbles in a star's motion. Barnard's Star, about 6 light-years away from us, seems to have such a wobble. It probably has two planets the size of Jupiter.

What does a light telescope do?

A light telescope is an instrument that makes it possible for scientists to study the stars. Far distant stars, viewed through a telescope, appear brighter and nearer.

The giant telescopes scientists use to study stars are called reflectors. The reflector telescope uses a mirror to gather light. It is focused into an image. When the image of a star is seen through the lens of a giant telescope, it can look a million times brighter than to the eye alone.

Which is the largest light telescope on Earth?

It is the 6-meter (236-inch) reflector in the U.S.S.R. Its mirror is so huge that as many as 40 people could stand on it. The second largest telescope is the 200-inch (5-meter) reflector at the Hale Observatories in California.

Observatory housing 6-meter Russian telescope. *Inset:* Largest light telescope.

How far can the giant telescopes see?

Giant telescopes have seen a quasar (KWAY-zahr) that scientists think is 15 billion light-years away from us.

Mysterious, brilliant spots mark the farthest edge of space we can see. They are called quasars. Quasars seem to be much smaller than galaxies, but thousands of times brighter.

What is Space Telescope?

Space Telescope is a 10-ton (9,100-kilogram) package with a 94-inch (2.4 meter) telescope and other equipment for looking into space *from space*. It will circle Earth high above our air and clouds. From there, Space Telescope will be able to see much farther and better than from Earth, where air and clouds block some of the view.

After Space Telescope is launched in 1983, it will be operated by remote control from Earth for at least 10 years. Astronauts will keep it in good condition. They can bring it back to Earth if necessary. Perhaps it will give us our first look at another planetary system.

Paintings of Space Telescope being released into Earth orbit from Space Shuttle.

Can humans look into a past time?

Yes. Every time you look at the stars, you see something that happened in the past. For example, Sirius (SEER-ee-us), the brightest star in the winter sky, is 9 light-years away. Starlight leaves Sirius, travels 9 years, and finally reaches our eyes. That starlight tells you what Sirius looked like *9 years ago.* To see what Sirius looks like *now,* you will have to wait another 9 years!

Pictures of galaxies that are billions of light-years away from us show how those galaxies looked billions of years ago.

How old is the Milky Way Galaxy?

It is about 10 billion years old. The universe is much older than that and Earth is much younger.

Imagine the age of the universe as one calendar year. The universe would begin on January 1. The Milky Way would appear on May 1. Earth would appear September 1. Humans would appear just before midnight on December 31!

Galaxy.

Do stars ever explode?

Yes. An exploding star is called a supernova. The exploding star may shine a billion times brighter than normal.

The most famous supernova was seen in the constellation Taurus (TAWR-us) in 1054 A.D. Chinese written records and North American Indian cave pictures tell us about the brilliant star that remained visible for two years.

The last supernova seen in our galaxy shone in 1604. Supernovas have been photographed in other galaxies. Sometimes they shine as brightly as their whole galaxy.

Crab nebula in Taurus.

What is left after a star explodes?

A large cloud of gas and dust plus a solid core is left behind. The cloud spreads out into space. It may be used to form new stars, planets, and living things.

Photographs taken with giant telescopes show a huge crab-shaped swirling cloud called the Crab Nebula spreading out from the site of the famous supernova of 1054 A.D.

What is a pulsar?

A pulsar is a star that sends out regular radio signals, or pulses. It is the solid core that remains after a star explodes. The pulsar in the Crab Nebula pulses 30 times a second.

The first pulsar, discovered in 1967, was nicknamed L.G.M. for **Little Green Men**. At first, scientists hoped the radio signals were coming from space creatures. But then other pulsars were found. Now we know that pulsar radio signals are natural and not caused by space creatures.

Do galaxies crash into each other?

Yes, but not very often. Several hundred photographs from the giant telescopes look like colliding galaxies or galaxies heading for collisions.

What would happen to you if another galaxy crashed into ours?

Probably nothing. Two galaxies can pass right through each other with few, if any, stars colliding. The stars in each galaxy are very far apart. Astronomers have never seen even one star or planet crash into another. So, probably no one on Earth—including you—would be affected at all if another galaxy crashed into ours.

Galaxy in Ursa Major.

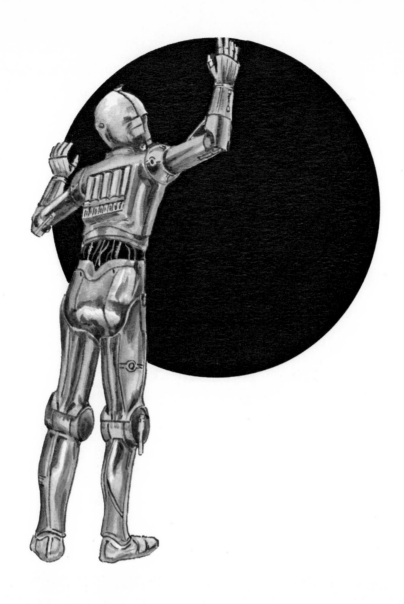

What is a black hole?

A black hole is not really a hole at all. It is a huge star that's been squeezed into a small ball. This star's gravity pulls things toward it billions of times more powerfully than Earth's gravity does. The pull of that powerful gravity traps everything, even light, inside the star. Since no light can escape, the star is invisible. That's why it's called a black hole in space.

Can we see a black hole?

A black hole can never be seen, so astronomers look for its effects on stars they *can* see. A black hole may suck material in from a nearby star. The falling gas from that star sends out X-rays at the edge of the black hole. These X-rays can be tracked.

In 1972, a spacecraft circling Earth found space X-rays coming from a spot called Cygnus (SIG-niss) X-1. Cygnus X-1 seems to be the first black hole ever found.

Could a passing spaceship be sucked into a black hole?

Anything passing too near a black hole would be sucked in by its mighty gravity. Whatever entered a black hole would be destroyed. If a passing spaceship were trapped in a black hole, it could never escape.

Can rockets fly to the stars?

No. Rockets must take along enough fuel for their entire space trip. A really long trip would need so much fuel that the rocket would be too heavy to fly. Apollo spacecraft flew astronauts to the moon at 25,000 miles an hour. At that speed, a trip to the closest stars would take thousands of years!

Lift-off of Apollo 16 Saturn V.

Rosette nebula in Monoceros.

What is the fastest a galactic cruiser could ever go?

Nothing can go faster than light. Starlight travels through empty space at 186,282 miles (299,800 kilometers) a second. We can't build a galactic cruiser today that travels through space at light-speed. But we can dream about building one in the future!

How long would a galactic cruiser take to travel to the stars?

Flying at the speed of light, a galactic cruiser could arrive at Proxima Centauri, our sun's nearest neighbor star, in a little more than 4 years. But most stars we see in the night sky are much, much farther away. A galactic cruiser racing at light-speed would take 782 years to reach Polaris, the North Star!

Painting of spacecraft powered by solar sail.

What could power a galactic cruiser?

A future galactic cruiser might scoop up hydrogen gas from space as it traveled. The hydrogen gas could be used to create nuclear energy. This would allow the cruiser to reach the fastest possible speed. Or a galactic cruiser might have a gigantic solar sail, which would catch sunlight. The sunlight would provide energy to move the cruiser.

There might be sources of power in space that no one has found yet. Humans have always dreamed of sailing out to the stars. Maybe in the 21st century they will.

Are there force fields in space?

Yes. There are force fields around stars and planets and in the vast spaces between them. An example is the gravity field that circles Earth. Earth's gravity field pulls things in toward Earth's center. Earth is also surrounded by a magnetic field. It is the magnetic field that causes compasses to move.

Can force fields affect the way you feel?

Yes. Since you live on Earth, you are used to the force field of Earth's gravity. But if you left Earth, you would be affected by different force fields. Our moon's gravity is much weaker than Earth's. If you visited the moon, you would feel very light. You could jump extra high. Jupiter's gravity is much stronger than Earth's. If you went there, you would feel much heavier.

Scientists in the Soviet Union report that people exposed to very strong electric and magnetic force fields (microwave radiation) can't think as well as usual. They get headaches and become tired, cranky, and forgetful.

What is a laser?

A laser is a device that sends out very strong beams of light. Laser beams are a pure color, narrow, and straight. Their enormous energy can be focused onto a small spot. Laser beams are so powerful that they can burn a hole in steel.

Can laser beams help humans?

Yes, in many different ways. Doctors use laser beams to perform operations. Machinists trim and join metals with laser beams. Surveyors measure distances on land with lasers. Scientists beamed light from a laser on Earth to a reflector left on the moon by the Apollo astronauts. It measured the exact distance to the moon.

Three-dimensional images called holograms are made by laser beams. Holograms make better pictures for science, medicine, or TV and movies. They can also be used to store many facts on one small piece of film.

Can laser beams kill humans?

Powerful laser beams can be death rays if their energy is focused on a person. Lasers must be used very carefully.

Laser.

Hologram.

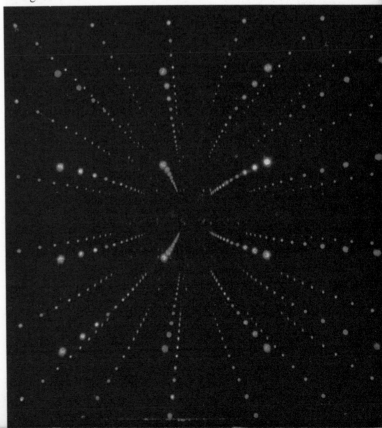

Photo of United States Skylab space station taken from command module.

What is a space station?

A space station is a structure that circles Earth high above our air and clouds. It can be a space lab where scientists may find out how people and things are affected by long stays in space. It can be an observation center for looking down at Earth or out to the stars. Future space stations may be used to launch starships to unknown worlds.

Cosmonauts do medical research on the Salyut space station.

Do space stations exist now?

Yes. The busiest space station so far is the Soviet Salyut 6. Russian astronauts, called cosmonauts, are stationed there for science experiments and observations. Supplies, fuel, and equipment are rocketed to the station as needed. The world's record for the longest stay in space was set in Salyut 6. Cosmonauts lived inside it for more than 4 months.

What is "zero g"?

"Zero g" stands for zero gravity. It means weightlessness. On Earth, gravity pulls everything in toward the center of the planet. Everything has weight. When you drop something, it falls to the ground.

Inside spacecraft circling Earth objects seem weightless. They are said to be in "zero g." When you drop something, it floats. Astronauts float too if they're not attached to the craft.

Humans are used to Earth's gravity. Zero g affects our minds and bodies. Some astronauts feel sick at first when they circle Earth inside spacecraft. They cannot work as quickly or as well as usual. They must do special exercises to keep in good physical condition.

What is a space colony?

A space colony will be a place away from Earth where thousands of people can live. Scientists are planning space colonies for the 21st century that will circle Earth thousands of miles out in space. Everything humans need to live normal lives will be available there.

Astronaut Edward H. White II floats in zero g while attached to the Gemini 4 spacecraft.

Will space colonies have gravity?

Space colonies will spin to create artificial gravity inside. The spinning will give everything weight. It will make space colonists feel just as well as they would on Earth.

Above: Painting of exterior of space colony. Disk above will reflect sunlight onto panels.

Can humans spend their entire lives in space?

Humans can live their lifetimes inside a space structure if their needs are taken care of. People need air, water, food, and artificial gravity. They must be protected from deadly radiation in space. No one knows yet how our bodies and minds will be affected by very long stays in space. So our first space colony will have living conditions as close as possible to those on Earth.

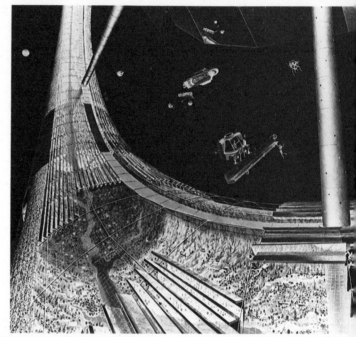

Above and below: Paintings of interiors of an earthlike space colony.

Painting of interior of an earthlike space colony.

What will our first space colony be like?

NASA pictures a space colony that humans could build in 22 years. Shaped like a wheel, it has room for 10,000 people inside. It circles Earth 250,000 miles out in space—as far away as the moon! The structure keeps spinning to create artificial gravity inside.

The space colony has its own air sealed in tight against space. It carries its own water supply, which can be cleaned and used over and over again. Sunshine provides light and power. A large turning paddle helps remove heat that is not needed.

Babies will be born, children will go to school, and adults will work in the space colony. It will have homes, schools, hospitals, and stores. Farms will provide plants and animals for food. There will be factories where clothes and other necessities will be made.

If we started this project right away, humans could have a colony in space soon after the year 2000!

57

Do we have a space freighter?

Our first space freighter, Space Shuttle, is expected to make frequent trips to and from space in the 1980s. It is as big as a jet plane, with plenty of room for cargo. One of its uses could be to travel to a space station. It could take new crews there and bring old ones home. It could carry new supplies and equipment to the space station.

Space Shuttle blasts off into space like a rocket. A large fuel tank is on the outside and is dropped off after launch. The fuel tank falls back into Earth's atmosphere and breaks up over a deserted ocean area. Two solids rocket boosters parachute down to the water. They are picked up so that they can be reused.

Space Shuttle circles Earth for 7 to 30 days on one mission. When the work is done, it returns to Earth and lands like an airplane. Each Shuttle will be used more than 100 times.

Photo of a Space Shuttle test flight.

What kind of missions can Space Shuttle fly?

Space Shuttle can take people and materials into space. Astronauts can go outside to check and repair satellites that are circling Earth. They can change film in the Space Telescope. They can build power stations to change sunlight into electricity for use on Earth.

Space Shuttle can carry a whole laboratory called Spacelab. Inside the lab everything will be at zero g. Scientists from many nations will do experiments there, trying to improve life for humans.

Painting of Space Shuttle crew member wearing a backpack that will propel the wearer.

How big is Space Shuttle's crew?

A crew can include up to seven men and women. A pilot flies the spacecraft. A mission specialist is in charge of equipment. One to four payload (cargo) specialists do the special work each mission needs.

The crew and passengers live in a two-level cabin in the front of the Shuttle. Controls are on the upper level. Seating and living areas are on the lower level. The cargo is held in the large space in the back.

Painting of astronauts constructing a solar power satellite.

Model of a personal rescue enclosure.

Will Shuttle passengers be able to escape in an emergency?

Shuttle carries life preservers for emergencies. These are large plastic balls that can be inflated. The air inside the balls has a temperature and a pressure like Earth's. People can breathe and stay warm in them. Each rescue ball measures almost 3 feet (86 centimeters) across. Since only one person fits inside, it is called a personal rescue enclosure.

If Shuttle has an emergency in space, each passenger will get inside a personal rescue enclosure. The pilot and mission specialist will put on spacesuits and help the passengers escape to a rescue ship.

How can you become a space explorer?

If you hope to explore space someday, you need to be in top physical and mental condition. Men and women have to be between 60 and 76 inches (152 and 193 centimeters) tall. Astronaut pilots and mission specialists must have a degree in engineering, mathematics, or science. Pilots must be experienced in flying jet planes. Mission specialists must be expert in their field.

People chosen to become space explorers must go through special training to prepare for their space missions. Space explorers know that they are part of one of the most exciting projects in human history!